FARM ANIMALS
Cows

by Sheri Doyle

Consulting Editor: Gail Saunders-Smith, PhD

Consultant: Dr. Celina Johnson, College of Agriculture
California State University, Chico

CAPSTONE PRESS
a capstone imprint

Pebble Plus is published by Capstone Press,
1710 Roe Crest Drive, North Mankato, Minnesota 56003.
www.capstonepub.com

Library of Congress Cataloging-in-Publication Data
Doyle, Sheri.
Cows / by Sheri Doyle.
p. cm.—(Pebble plus. Farm animals)
Includes bibliographical references and index.
Summary: "Simple text and full-color photographs provide a brief introduction to cows"—Provided by publisher.
ISBN 978-1-4296-8646-4 (library binding)
ISBN 978-1-62065-299-2 (ebook PDF)
1. Dairy cattle—Juvenile literature. 2. Cows—Juvenile literature. I. Title.
SF208.D69 2013
636.2—dc23   2011049856

Editorial Credits
Erika L. Shores, editor; Ashlee Suker, designer; Marcie Spence, media researcher; Eric Manske, production specialist

Photo Credits
Alamy Images: blickwinkel, 21; Shutterstock: AGphotographer, 13, alek.k, 9, basketman23, 17, Elenamiv, design
element, Jane Rix, 7, Kookkai_nak, design element, Linda Armstrong, 19, Phillip W. Kirkland, 15, Simon Krzic, 11,
tepic, cover, 1, verityjohnson, 5

Note to Parents and Teachers

The Farm Animals series supports national science standards related to life science. This book
describes and illustrates cows. The images support early readers in understanding the text. The
repetition of words and phrases helps early readers learn new words. This book also introduces
early readers to subject-specific vocabulary words, which are defined in the Glossary section.
Early readers may need assistance to read some words and to use the Table of Contents,
Glossary, Read More, Internet Sites, and Index sections of the book.

Printed in the United States of America in North Mankato, Minnesota.
042012   006682CGF12

Table of Contents

Meet the Cows

Moo! It's early morning
on the farm. Here come
some spotted cows!
They walk on hooves
and sway their tails.

Cows have wide muzzles
and big ears. Cows have
short or long hair that is black,
white, brown, red, or gray.
Some cows are spotted.

One dairy cow weighs about 1,500 pounds (680 kilograms). That's as heavy as two motorcycles!

Grazing Days

Cows eat grass, hay,

and grain. Cows burp up

their swallowed food as cud.

Cows chew cud

for eight hours a day.

A cow drinks 30 gallons
(114 liters) of water each day.
That's enough to fill a bathtub.
Cows drink from ponds,
streams, or tanks.

New Life

A calf is born! It stands

within 30 minutes.

It's an adult after one year.

Cows can live for

15 to 20 years.

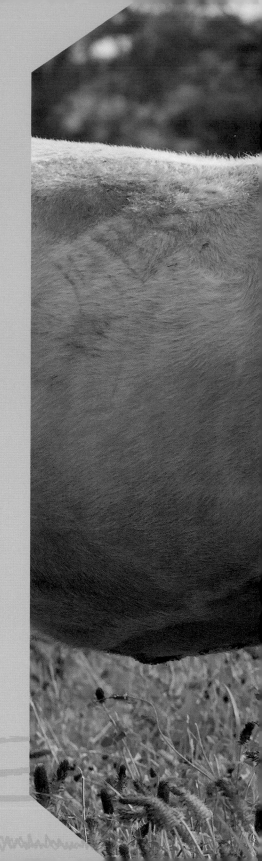

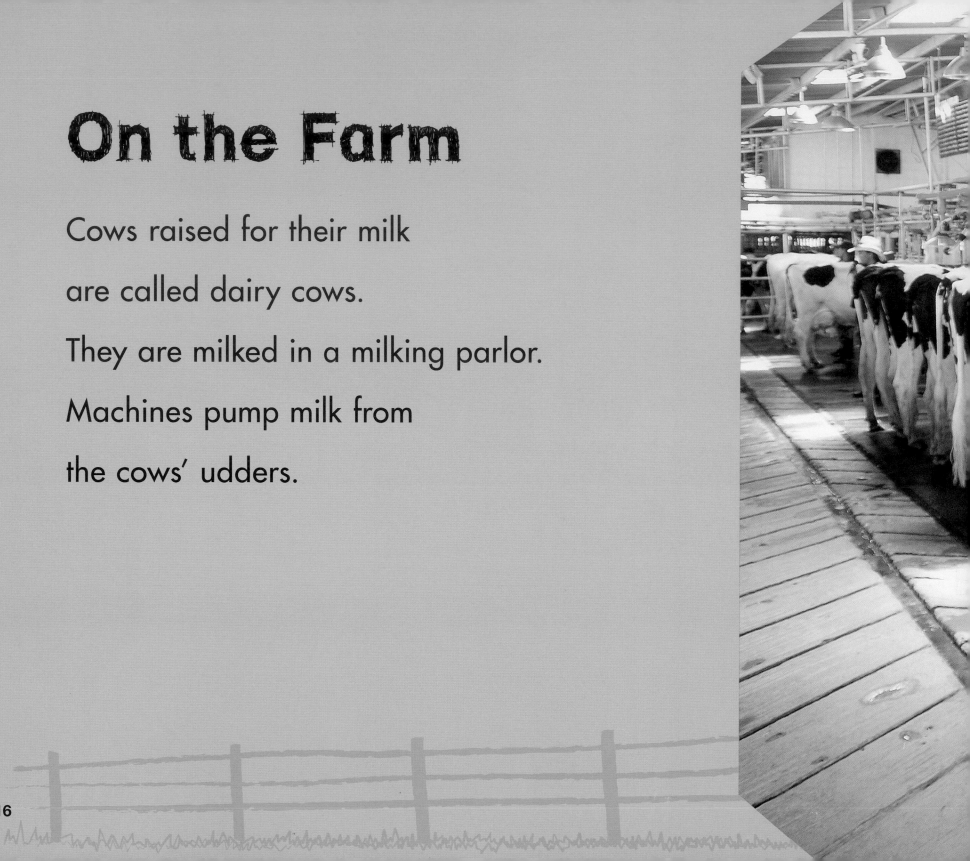

On the Farm

Cows raised for their milk

are called dairy cows.

They are milked in a milking parlor.

Machines pump milk from

the cows' udders.

udder

Beef cows are raised for meat.
Their hides are used to
make shoes, baseball gloves,
and many other products.

Cows might sleep in barns

when it's very cold, hot,

or stormy. They snooze

in grassy areas called pastures

the rest of the time.

in barns

d, hot,

ooze

alled pastures

e.

udder

Beef cows are raised for meat.
Their hides are used to
make shoes, baseball gloves,
and many other products.

Glossary

cud—swallowed food that is burped back into a cow's mouth and chewed again

dairy cow—a female cow that produces milk

grain—plant seeds such as barley, corn, oats, and wheat

graze—to eat grass

hay—dried grass used to feed cows

hoof—a cow's foot; more than one hoof is hooves

muzzle—the nose, mouth, and lower part of a cow's face

pasture—a grassy area of land that cows and other animals feed upon

udder—the body part that fills with milk and hangs under a cow

Read More

Diemer, Laura. *Cows.* Watch Them Grow. New York: Weigl Publishers, 2011.

Macken, JoAnn Early. *Cows.* Animals That Live on the Farm. Pleasantville, N.Y.: Weekly Reader, 2010.

Stockland, Patricia M. *In the Cattle Yard.* Barnyard Buddies. Edina, Minn.: Magic Wagon, 2008.

Internet Sites

FactHound offers a safe, fun way to find Internet sites related to this book. All of the sites on FactHound have been researched by our staff.

Here's all you do:

Visit *www.facthound.com*

Type in this code: 9781429686464

Check out projects, games and lots more at
www.capstonekids.com

Index

Word Count: 195
Grade: 1
Early-Intervention Level: 14